GRAY WHALES

Jim Darling

WORLDLIFE LIBRARY

Voyageur Press

Contents

Introduction

I first came across gray whales while surfing through the summers off Long Beach on the west coast of Vancouver Island, British Columbia. Friends and I would be lounging outside the surf breaks named 'Tiny's' or 'The Rock',

watching for incoming swells, or in the midst of paddling out, dodging and diving through the breaking waves, when a whale would suddenly blow close enough to stop our hearts. It got our attention. We were on the edge of flight until we could be sure it wasn't the local killer whales – which had a history of closely examining wet-suited, seal-sized creatures and scaring them near death – before someone would declare it a gray. Then with a deep collective breath, mixed with a little lingering wariness, we'd get back to surfing. It was nice actually, surfing with whales in our midst.

A young gray whale surfaces, mouth open, with cream-coloured baleen visible.

From then on I continued to encounter gray whales. While driving charter boats in the area sighting gray whales became such a regular occurrence that I began to search for information about them. Not only was there little to find, what there was said gray whales weren't even supposed to be off Vancouver Island in the summer. They were all supposed to be in the Bering Sea. At the same time I began to realize we were seeing the same individual whales over and over again. They were recognizable by striking white pigment patterns on their gray backs – one had a white teardrop,

The eye of a newborn gray whale.

Gray whales have a dark overall coloring, mixed with a variety of mottled white patterns, giving an impression of gray. They have a smooth back with no dorsal fin. Photographs of these skin patterns are used by researchers to identify individual whales, and keep records of their behavior.

another had two large circles, and so on. A photo-ID catalog of the Vancouver Island gray whales was soon established, and became a basis for studies that I'm still involved in 25 years later.

Those early whales all had names, 'Two Dot Star', 'Whitepatch', 'Big White', 'Blackjack', 'Squirl' and others. Many of them returned to our area, clearly their summer home range, year after year. One in particular, Two Dot Star, has returned every year since the mid 1970s, making him at least 25 years old and something of an old friend.

Two Dot Star, (which we sometimes shorten to TDS) returns each spring, presumably after the winter breeding season in Mexico. He breaks from the northward migration to haunt the shallow sandy bays along the island's west coast. His skin markings, which initially excited us when they hadn't changed over two years, are still crystal clear after more than twenty, although his entire body has grown a little whiter. TDS seems to prefer bottom feeding – slurping in

A gray whale blows in the calm waters of its feeding grounds.

mouthfuls of sediment and filtering out small organisms – rather than chasing various plankton blooms that have become common prey for many of the grays in the region. I have, on occasion, seen him devour mysid plankton swarms, but he is not a kelp bed denizen – as many of the younger whales are today – and so he is most likely to appear when the bottom food is best.

If he is around we expect to see two or three other whales we've known for a while, but he also can be alone for extended periods. Two Dot Star was never a very sociable whale – nothing like the 'friendlies' that can be draped all over the boat with people kissing them on the nose. At best, Two Dot Star ignores us. If the boat happens to be close when he surfaces, fine, he will swim by, but he's pretty adept at keeping a distance. It was only a couple of years ago, through collecting a skin sample and genetic analysis that we confirmed he was male. With all the enormous changes over the last 25 years it is comfortable to run into TDS. I wonder if he knows he went from being a nonentity in the scientific literature to being a relatively well-studied whale, or that he went from officially endangered to officially recovered in that time – and is now subject to whaling again.

Gray whales, TDS and his kind, have a lot of 'firsts' and 'onlys' attached to them. They are the only species in their family, and are substantially different from the other baleen whales. They are the only whale species we know of where entire populations have become extinct. They were the first, along with right whales, to be protected by the International Whaling Commission (IWC) in 1937, meaning they had been the first along with right whales to be decimated by whaling. They were the first large whale to be 're-discovered' after World War II and, arguably, the initiators of the phenomenal public interest in whales that began in the 1960s. They are the only large whale to be held in captivity for extended periods – and released again. They are definitely the first aggressively 'friendly' whales, that is, the first to approach and rub on boats and let passengers pet them. They are the first to be declared recovered and taken off the endangered species lists and the first to be whaled again in non-arctic North America.

Within this book I hope to give you a feeling for the nature of the gray whale and our relationship with it. This whale lives closer to land, and to us, than any other large whale; and has the reputation among whalers of being the most vicious, cunning, and courageous – and to the rest of us, the most friendly…

A friendly gray whale positions itself to be touched.

Intertidal Whales

The whales bask on the shores in the rays of the sun.
– F E Beddard, 1900

This comment in *A Book of Whales*, written at the turn of the nineteenth century, is only the slightest of exaggerations. If I had to pick just one characteristic that distinguished gray whales from all the other baleen whales, it would be their extreme inshore, shallow water habits. At times they can be found in water levels waist deep. When surfing I couldn't believe whales would purposely be inside a surf break – but as it turns out they are at home there.

The comfort of gray whales with extreme shallows has clearly long astonished observers. Charles Scammon, the whaling captain who wrote some of the earliest descriptions of gray whales in 1869, commented, '…To our surprise, we saw numbers of these grays going through the surf where there could barely have been depth to float them. We could see in many places, by the white sand coming to the surface, that they must appear to be touching bottom. One in particular lay for half-an-hour in the breakers playing…' An account by C H Townsend in 1886 of the migrations includes, '…Gray whales then (1854) resorted to shoal water along the north beach of Monterey Bay to roll in the sand as a relief from the barnacles and other parasites which infested them, and were easily secured, especially when half stranded at low tide.' And at the other end of the gray whale world, Russian researchers B A Zenkovich and A G Tomilin described, in 1937, grays of the Koryak coast in Siberia, 'The whales entered the lagoons, and dozens of them filled the shallow lakes connected with the sea. Some whales were just lying on the sand bars: with the tide they would move out to sea, and begin to feed as if nothing had happened…'

These are not exceptional sightings. Grays can virtually live on the beach. At one point early on in my studies I was surveying Ahous Bay, a semi-protected bay with a long surf-swept sandy beach, on the west coast of Vancouver Island. It was a hot midsummer day with small 2–3 ft (0.5–1 m) breakers along the beach. I came across three whales inside the breakers, lying on their sides with most of their girth and one pectoral fin out of the water, wiggling back and forth with the waves breaking along their sides as if they were jetties. I nosed the boat in as much as I dared, convinced I had three stranded whales on my hands and about to call half the nearby town to see if we could set them free. I was about to put on a wetsuit when, with a couple of casual snake-like slithers, they backed out of the shallows, moved along the beach a short distance and made their way back into the breakers to repeat the activity. They were feeding on invertebrates in the sand, in water about 5 ft (1.5 m) deep – in the intertidal zone.

What makes a gray whale? Just like any other creature it has evolved with the environment or ecological niche it has come to occupy; this is largely the result of the food resource it utilizes. Gray whales feed predominantly on organisms buried in, or moving just above, bottom sediments, and at times on planktonic prey that concentrate in kelp beds or surf-zones found all along shorelines or on shallow offshore banks. This niche has led to a number of physical features and behavioral characteristics that are sufficiently unique for the gray whale to be the only member of its own family of baleen whales.

Whales can be divided into two types – those with teeth, known as the Odontocetes or toothed whales, and those which have lost their teeth and instead have a filtering apparatus in their mouths called baleen, known as the Mysticetes or baleen whales. The toothed whales include all the dolphins, killer whales and the largest toothed whale, the sperm whale. The baleen whales include all the other large whales you might be familiar with;

Gray whales often feed on small organisms (invertebrates) in bottom sediments.
They position the sides of their mouths against the sea floor and use suction to fill their mouths with
sand or mud. Then, using their tongues they push the sediments through their baleen filter, as shown in
this photograph, and swallow their prey. This whale is feeding on small shrimp that live in the mud.

Gray whales host masses of barnacles and parasitic cyamids (or whale lice) that can be found in congregations on their heads and backs. The barnacles filter the sea water for food and the whale lice feed on the whale's skin. The twin blowholes characteristic of all baleen whales produce the V-shaped exhalation.

the blue, fin, humpback, right and so on. The baleen whales are divided into four families based on their physical characteristics. These are: the Eschrichtiidae – which has only one species, the gray whale; the Balaenidae – the right and bowhead whales; the Neobalaenidae – the pygmy right whale; and lastly the Balaenopteridae – all the rest, including blues, fins, sei, Brydes, minke and humpbacks. The point to be made is that gray whales are on their own. They are different enough not only to warrant their own species, but their own family.

Gray whales are medium-sized baleen whales. As adults they can reach 39–50 ft (12–16 m) in length, compared to minke whales at a mere 23 ft (7 m) or blue whales at an impressive 98 ft (30 m) long. As with all baleen whales, the female is larger than the male. Historical records of measurements taken directly from hunted gray whales confirm this; for example, from 146 whales measured in Korea during the years 1911–12, the average size for females was 41 ft (12.5 m), and for males it was $38\frac{2}{3}$ ft (11.8 m); of 316 whales killed off the American coast in the 1960s, the average female size was 46 ft (14 m) and the average male size was $42\frac{1}{2}$ ft (13 m); of the 216 whales killed off Chukotka during 1977–81, the average size for females was 39 ft (12 m) and for males it was $37\frac{2}{3}$ ft (11.5 m). One circumference reported was 28–30 ft (c. 9 m), and pectorals have been measured at 6 ft (1.8 m) and flukes at 10 ft (3 m) across. One weight reported was for a 43.8 ft (13.4 m) female at 34.6 tons (without blood or fluids).

Two distinguishing physical characteristics make gray whales very difficult to mis-identify. Firstly, their color. Gray whales, unlike any other species of baleen whales, are decidedly a mottled gray, but with much variation in degree. Some are very dark with just a few gray markings, others are very light, the entire body being covered with blotches of white and gray so that overall they appear more white than black. In addition to the skin pigment patterns, the entire body of the gray is often thickly infested with whale lice and barnacles in orange or yellow-white patches.

The second characteristic is their form. Gray whales have a smooth upper back with no dorsal fin. However just behind the dorsal hump is a very distinctive set of bumps or 'knuckles' running along the top of the back to the fluke. If you clench your fist and look at the knuckles, you are looking at something very much like a gray whale's back. The pectoral fins are short and pointy compared to other whales. If a whale is mottled gray, has knuckles along its back instead of a dorsal fin, and is found within a few kilometres of the shore, it is certainly a gray whale.

Its physical attributes are not the only product of the animal's ecological niche. Its niche also governs annual cycles, behavior patterns, and ultimately social organization and communication. The gray whale's life is dramatically divided into two cycles, with huge migrations between one and the other. The summer is spent feeding in cold waters along the continental coastlines or shallow northern seas. Gray whales then make long migrations south to breeding grounds thousands of miles away. They stay for just weeks if mating, or for several months if giving birth and nursing the newborn, before heading north again. These patterns have ultimately been derived from prey availability and distribution, leading to female distributions and cycles that benefit survival of the young, and corresponding male distributions, mating seasons and systems.

Our knowledge of gray whale social organization is very limited. They appear to live in herd-like structures not dissimilar to large herds of land mammals such as caribou, buffalo or wildebeest. The longest known social bond is between mother and young, lasting for 6 to 7 months. However there are several hints that longer-term and more complex social relationships may exist. For example, the small group of whales that have returned to Vancouver Island each summer for over twenty years undoubtedly know each other as individuals, and their potential genetic relationship is

Perhaps the most conspicuous identifying characteristic of a gray whale is the series of 'knuckles' along its back behind its dorsal hump. These knuckles, lack of a dorsal fin and distinctive mottled coloring make identification of this species relatively easy.

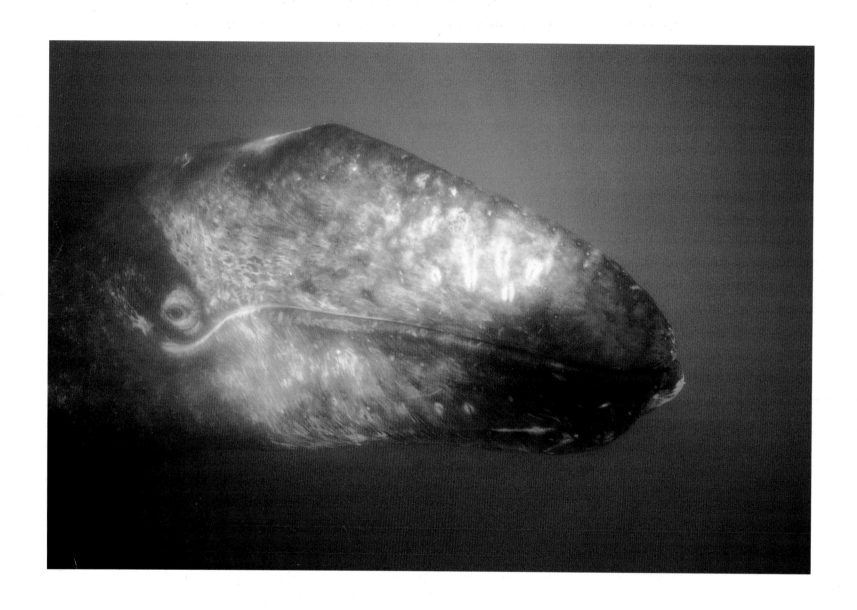

A gray whale calf peers at the photographer. Most calves are born in
traditional calving lagoons in Baja, Mexico during the winter. They measure between
13 to 16 ft (4 to 5 m) at birth. Like many young animals they can be very curious.

currently being studied. One wonders if such summer groups exist throughout the range. Accounts of males assisting each other in mating; the social interactions of newborn calves; stories told by whalers of males showing 'affection' for females – staying close to assist them when harpooned, sometimes until they are killed themselves; or accounts of observations in the breeding lagoons of an adult assisting the mother of a stranded calf by jointly rocking it off the sand bar, all hint at more complex relationships than are generally ascribed to grays.

Gray whales communicate with a variety of sounds, about which we know little. Early studies concluded that they made few if any sounds and even dubbed grays the 'quiet whale'. Further investigations have indicated that this is far from the case, and suggest the grays may be one of the most vocal of whales, especially between mother and young. It is probable that these mixed impressions arose because the calls they make are often of lower frequency than the background biological noise, itself often very heavy in the habitats they occupy. Gray whales produce a variety of low-frequency sounds, including moans, grunts, croaks, rumbles, and loud clicks or bangs. Virtually nothing is known of the function of these and only two have been attributed to any behavioral context. One researcher notes the most unusual and loudest sound is like the bong of a huge Chinese gong, preceded by a loud rasp, and suggests that this is an alert signal. Loud clicks or bangs have also been heard from calves or their mothers when they are separated in the lagoons.

Grays are shallow water whales. They range into lagoons, bays, river mouths, within the thinnest sliver of habitat along continental shorelines and in shallows of the northern seas. It is this which makes gray whales gray whales. Everything about them reflects this habitat, from the shape of their baleen to their calls. It is also the characteristic that brings them danger, as they are a little too accessible to their major predator – mankind.

Four Populations

Once there were four populations or herds of gray whales in the world. Then there were three, now there are two – just barely. Only one is healthy; the other is hanging on precariously. Gray whales hold the dubious distinction of being the only whale species with entire populations declared extinct.

At one time there were gray whale herds on either side of the North Atlantic and on either side of the North Pacific. Gray whales had one of the most limited geographical distributions of any species of baleen whale, being restricted to the Northern Hemisphere between the subtropics and the ice. In contrast, most other baleen species exist in both hemispheres and in all oceans of the world. How grays came to be distributed in two northern oceans so apparently separate and why they never occupied the southern oceans, are prehistoric mysteries. The likely explanation of the former is that at some warmer time grays moved through Arctic passages between the Atlantic and Pacific oceans. Today Pacific gray whales range substantial distances; to the west along the Siberian coastline and to the east along the North American Arctic coastline towards the Atlantic in summer; however trans-oceanic movement no longer occurs.

The European herd of gray whales apparently ranged at least through the North and Baltic Seas. Our knowledge of them comes from fossil and subfossil remains. Gray whale bones and partial skeletons have been found on the Swedish coast of the Gulf of Bothnia, in England off the coasts of Cornwall and Devon and in the Netherlands in a portion of the Zuiderzee drained in 1930. Seven finds in Europe dated from between 4000 BC and AD 500 led researchers to conclude grays occurred along the European coast in the first centuries AD. They seem to have disappeared in prehistoric times. What happened to gray whales in Europe is anyone's guess. Possibly they were whaled-out, as they lived well within reach of the Basque whaling culture that operated throughout parts of the North Atlantic in the eleventh and twelfth centuries.

The American Atlantic herd of gray whales ranged at least from Florida to New England, and possibly further north. Reports of gray whales arise from waters off Nantucket and Cape Cod. One mentions whales hunted in Delaware Bay that were not right whales and which were frequently grounded on shoals and bars, which strongly suggests they were gray whales. The first published report of what is probably a gray whale came in 1725 in an essay describing a whale seen along the New England coast. The author, Paul Dudley, reported a Scrag Whale which, from its description including, '… part of its back is scragged with half a dozen knobs or knuckles…', seems to describe a gray whale. The clearest evidence of this lost gray whale population comes from a series of bone specimens found along the eastern seaboard from the 1850s to the 1970s. Radio-carbon dating indicates these are between 300 and 10,000 years old. Clearly, through the 1600s gray whales occupied the American Atlantic shorelines; this population was likely gone by the end of the 1700s, its loss making gray whales extinct in the Atlantic Ocean.

In the Pacific, both herds of gray whales appear to have made it through to the next millennium – just. Both the eastern and western Pacific herds have been declared extinct at least once in the last 100 years but they seemed to have beaten the odds. The eastern Pacific or American herd that ranges from Mexico to Siberia is also often called the California or Chukotka-California stock. The western Pacific herd ranges along the Asian coast and is also called the Okhotsk-Korean population. Most investigators have felt there is no ongoing connection between the two stocks; however, considering the current remnant status of the Asian herd and well-known mobility of large whales, this remains an open question. Genetic comparisons to determine the relationship between these stocks are currently underway.

A gray whale breaches in the Mexican breeding lagoons. The whales may jump clear of the water to land on their sides or backs once or dozens of times in a row. The purpose of this behavior is not clear, as it occurs in many different geographical and social situations. Possibilities include it as a form of communication, a reaction to a social encounter with other whales, or sheer exuberance.

The Asian population ranged from the northern shores of the Sea of Okhotsk and the Kamchatka peninsula southwards to the southern Korean and Japanese coast and to breeding areas that have not been well defined. Their range may extend further south to China or even Vietnam. Prior to commercial whaling, estimates of the number of whales in this population were 1500–10,000 whales. Grays were the subject of traditional whaling along the southern coasts of Japan, but the numbers taken were most likely few in comparison to the size of the herd. However, during the first half of the 1900s Asian grays were subject to intensive whaling from Korean shore stations as well as from American, Japanese, Norwegian and Soviet Union vessels. Few remained after the 1930s and by the 1950s it was felt that none of these gray whales remained. The 1960s and 70s brought only scattered sightings of one or two at a time in Russian and Japanese waters, with some estimates in the 1980s suggesting that perhaps 100–200 grays may have survived. Sightings during the 1990s of grays passing off the Japan Pacific coast, and of as many as 200 in the Russian Sakilin Island region, have revived hope for the future of this population.

The remaining gray whale population, the eastern Pacific herd, seems worlds apart from its three cousins. Ranging between its winter calving lagoons of Baja, Mexico and feeding grounds along the North American coast and in Bering, Chukchi and Arctic Seas, it appears to be a robust, healthy whale population. Thought to be near extinct in the 1930s it has made a comeback to the estimated pre-whaling numbers of more than 20,000. With its migration (heralded as one of the world's great wildlife spectacles) within sight of the population centers of the American west coast, it has become one of the most observed, studied, best known and loved whale populations in the world. This is the population the remainder of the book is about.

A recently born calf showing its few mammalian hair follicles.

'So Constantly and Variously Pursued'

The civilized whaler seeks the hunted animal farther seaward, as from year to year it learns to shun the fatal shore. No species of the whale tribe is so constantly and variously pursued as the one we have endeavored to describe, and the large bays and lagoons where once these animals congregated, brought forth and nurtured their young, are now nearly deserted. Their mammoth bones lie bleaching on the shores of those placid waters, and were strewn along the broken coasts from Eastern Siberia to the Gulf of California. Ere long the California Gray will be known only as one of the extinct species of cetacea recorded in history…
– Charles Scammon 1869

Perhaps the most amazing thing about this quote is that it refers to the eastern Pacific gray whale population that recovered. Imagine what happened to the others that are gone. After looking through gray whaling history the question becomes not how did gray whale populations become extinct – but how in the world did any survive?

Since ancient times gray whales were prey to certain native peoples around the Pacific rim from Japan to North America. They were hunted by the Japanese, the native inhabitants of Kamchatka Koryak regions and the Chukotka Peninsula on the Siberian coast, the Aluets and Eskimos in Alaska and the Nu Chal Nuth of the west coast of Vancouver Island and the Olympic Peninsula in Washington State. Many of these peoples hold a long cultural history of whaling with grays as one of their quarry – no doubt the result of the extreme inshore habits of the animals. Currently, the aboriginal hunt of grays continues on the Siberian coast, and is now also underway off the Olympic Peninsula. It is difficult to estimate how many grays were taken by the native peoples, but at the peak and throughout their range it is doubtful it exceeded a few hundred a year. Whatever the numbers were, they were limited by need and opportunity.

The slaughter came from elsewhere. The majority of the herd of California gray whales congregated in protected lagoons on the west coast of Mexico for several months each winter to calve and breed. It has been described as a whalers' haven. Here they could spend the winter anchored in protected lagoons in a mild climate, with whales so thick you could walk on them.

Whaling ships first entered breeding lagoons at Magdalena Bay in 1846 and two years later, in 1848, at least twenty ships anchored there between December and March. An intense period of whaling followed, and thousands of whales were killed. By all accounts, even with whalers still relying on hand harpoons from skiffs, this was a massacre. A few lines from Charles Scammon the whaling captain, who in 1858 'discovered' and first whaled in the nearby Laguna Ojo de Liebre (or Scammon's Lagoon), provide the picture: '…two or three calves have been seen with one whale, but these instances have only occurred in lagoons where there had been great slaughter among the cows, leaving their offspring motherless, which straggle about, sometimes following other whales, or congregating by themselves, a half a dozen together at times.' About a decade after this the lagoons were all but empty. In 1867, two whaling ships searched the Magdalena Bay for two months and captured only two whales. By the 1870s the lagoon whaling was over – for a while.

Whaling had not stopped, however. Shore whaling stations along the coast of California were still operating. As one author of the day, C H Townsend, explained, '…small boats could be sent out to capture gray whales during their annual migrations which permitted the business being continued so cheaply it was still profitable.' During 1886 it was reported that 167 grays were caught in three seasons by California shore stations, '…a very fair showing for a species so scarce in 1880 that only one individual could be captured.' But by the early 1900s shore whaling in California was

A very young calf, approximately 13 ft (4 m) in length, lifts its eye above the water in a Mexican calving lagoon. One indication of its young age is the absence of barnacles and whale lice that will soon appear. At about two months of age this calf will migrate thousands of miles to northern feeding grounds.

A whale checks its observers. Gray whales were relentlessly hunted until their
international protection in 1946. The only population that has recovered to near pre-whaling abundance
ranges along the North American west coast and into the Bering and Chukchi Seas.

obsolete as the whales had become so scarce.

This unrelenting pursuit, though still relying on hand harpoons and skiffs, decimated the eastern Pacific herd of gray whales. Original numbers are estimated at between 20,000–40,000. We have no idea how few whales were left after it became unprofitable to hunt them, but they must have reached their lowest levels during the last decade of the 1800s. They had disappeared from our view. One noted whale scientist, Roy Chapman Andrews, commented in 1914, '…during the past twenty years the species has been lost to science and many naturalists believed it to be extinct…'

It was not. Why or how, is one of those pleasant unknowns – but apparently the whalers missed a few. Later documentation of other breeding lagoons on the mainland Mexican coast that were not whaled may be part of the answer. In 1921, however, gray whales were rare enough that a single sighting warranted a publication in the *Journal of Mammalogy*: in March 1921 two California gray whales, 'under conditions that rendered identification beyond question,' were northbound, 20 miles (32 km) south of San Diego.

So, astonishing as it might seem today, lagoon whaling began again. This time it was by modern factory ships in Magdalena Bay where, during the 1925–26 whaling season, they noted the reappearance of gray whales and killed 42 of them. Whaling statistics for grays along the North American coast tell the story better than any words. From 1919–1929, 234 gray whales were taken commercially off western North America. In the years 1925–29, in the breeding grounds, 222 were taken, in dramatically declining numbers: 140 in 1925; 42 in 1926; 29 in 1927; nine in 1928; and two in 1929. Then another seven were taken along the coast from California to Alaska. By 1930 investigators were again warning that the status of gray whales was extremely critical, and were concerned that only a few dozen individuals survived in the eastern Pacific.

Gray whales of the North American coast have the distinction of being presumed near extinction twice within a 50-year period. If they had been making any comeback at all since lagoon whaling of the 1800s they were definitely deterred from 1924–1929 when the lagoons were all but cleaned out for a second time. The difference the second time was that the threat of extinction existed on both sides of the Pacific – as whaling in the early 1900s had crushed the Asian population as well. Protective agreements were passed by the International Whaling Commission in 1937 and although gray whaling stopped along the North American coast at this time, this agreement was not adhered to by the Soviet Union and Japan until 1946. Finally, 100 years after the first lagoon whaling, we stopped killing gray whales… but it was not totally clear if there were any left to be subjects of protection.

Seemingly a population with nine lives, some had again survived along the North American coastline. Scattered reports through the late 1930s and the 1940s tell us a few still frequented our coasts through the World War II years: enough to make a comeback. The modern revival of interest in gray whales, and arguably whales in general, may have been initiated by Carl Hubbs who, with his students, in the daylight hours between December 1946 and February 1947 was able to count an 'astounding total of 200 gray whales passing La Jolla California moving south'. This realization that gray whales were indeed not extinct but present in significant numbers opened the doors to a phenomenal era of interest in whales.

With protection from hunting, and a built-in resiliency that defies description, the gray whale population has prospered. The estimates of population size have increased from 2500–3000 in the 1950s, to over 20,000 in the 1990s, perhaps nearing pre-whaling abundance. With this has come a proportional increase in public interest, such that gray whales now engage millions of people annually – in the pursuit of simply watching them.

Spray from water blasted into the air with its exhalation showers the broad back of an adult gray – a whale that may reach a length of 46 ft (14 m).

Desert Whales

Each winter, from January through March, the majority of the eastern Pacific herd of gray whales congregate in the shallow protected lagoons along the west coast of Baja, Mexico. The largest and most famous of the breeding lagoons from south to north are, Magdalena, San Ignacio and Ojo de Libre. These, once the primary sites of lagoon whaling in the 1800 and early 1900s, again host the largest numbers of whales. During the winter months gray whales are distributed from San Diego, California, all along the Baja coast to Cabo San Lucas and across to the Mexican mainland coast.

This winter destination led to one of the gray whale's many nicknames – the 'desert whale'. Here the Baja desert with its rugged brown mountains, cactus forests and dried lake beds, dips slightly and blends right into the turbid shallow lagoons, which are just crammed with whales. If one enters from the sea in late January, the narrow, at times surf-swept channels are alive with hundreds, if not thousands, of whales. Back-lit, the blows are so numerous it looks like a series of long sprinkler hoses with holes down the lengths. If approaching from land, the first sight is the far reaches of the lagoons and the tranquil blows of cows with newborn calves. These are the breeding grounds, for mating, birth and the nursing of newborn.

This is a short period of the year for gray whales. Little feeding occurs. The lagoons may be occupied for three months, but much of the activity is over in six weeks or less, leaving only the cows with newborn calves to linger. During this intense period, grays distributed over thousands of miles from California to Siberia during the rest of the year, coalesce. Two quite separate and, preferably for females, mutallly exclusive activities occur here. Mating congregations occur near the entrances to the lagoons, whereas

An adult gray whale lifts its head from San Ignacio Lagoon, Baja, Mexico.

birth and nursing of newborn calves occurs in the inner lagoons. Immature whales may be spread throughout. Why grays make this migration and assemble in Mexico is not entirely clear, as not all whale species behave this way. Certainly the mixing of the majority of the herd is achieved, and birth occurs under conditions that presumably benefit the young, which would otherwise be born in colder, deeper, rougher seas, within easier grasp of killer whales.

Gray whale aggregation in the breeding lagoons.

Lagoon mating activity occurs predominantly over a brief period in January. The collective estrus of females may occur over a shorter period than is the case with many other whales. Some researchers, their information based on an extensive examination of the ovaries of a series of dead gray females, suggest that most conceptions actually occur within a three-week period in the southern migration in late November and early December. This would make the activity in the lagoon entrances of a secondary nature, possibly involving females that have not yet conceived and are undergoing a second estrus cycle. Whether the activity in the lagoon entrances in late January is primary or secondary, it is frantic.

The scene is one of hundreds of whales in loose aggregation at the lagoon entrances, with groups of two, three, up to 15 or more in tight groups rolling over and rubbing on each other, flippers and flukes flailing around and

One whale sliding over the back of another; possibly in a mating group.
Mating occurs over a several week period in aggregations of adults at lagoon
entrances. Often several males mate with one female in succession. It is thought the
order of mating and/or amount of sperm determines which male is successful.

A newborn gray, 13–16 ft (4–5 m) long, born during the southward migration off Monterey, California. Most calves are born in the protected Baja lagoons in Mexico where they can reside for several months before the migration north. Calf mortality can be high, mainly due to strandings and attacks by killer whales.

thrashing the surface. As whales roll horizontally, extended pink penes are often visible. Some descriptions suggest gray whale mating involves two males and a female. The second male is presumed to assist or stabilize the female. This behavior is not well understood and gives rise to some theoretical questions – why would one male be helping another? It is clear, however, that several males may mate with an estrus female. Mating bouts may last for several hours, with some whales leaving and others joining over the duration. There is a marked absence of overt fighting or competition between males, leaving the impression they essentially take turns with cooperative females. The presumption is that sperm competition occurs after a mating session with multiple males, with the order and quantity of sperm determining which male actually fertilizes the egg. The mating system is a poorly known aspect of gray whale behavior, and is a subject begging for study. It is apparently a system tuned to a very short simultaneous estrus of many females, with male behavior patterns having evolved accordingly. By the end of January to early February mating activity wanes, with many of the newly pregnant females and mature males leaving the winter grounds to migrate northwards again.

Mothers-to-be follow a different schedule. Most females produce a calf every other year. The gestation period is 12 to 13 months. Late pregnant females return to the lagoons a year after mating, with most births occurring in a 5 to 6 week period, the peak occurring between mid and late January. Several births have been observed, with the 13–16-ft- (4–5-m) long calf emerging from the mother, immediately taking breaths by itself, and within a matter of hours swimming like other young whales in the lagoons. Cows and newly born calves are usually solitary, occupying the further calm reaches of the lagoons, especially through the first part of the season when mating activities are underway. One researcher commented that there is almost a whale-free buffer zone between courting whales nearest the inlet and mother-young pairs deepest within the lagoon interior. The mothers and calves are primarily engaged in resting and nursing and this separation provides a degree of protection from harassment by courting whales.

The first few months of lagoon life are critical to the survival of the calf. Several stages of calf development have been described in 1987 by researchers Steve Swartz and Mary Lou Jones. Newborn calves lack coordination and endurance and stay very close to a protective mother. As they grow a little older they move from upper reaches to lower in the lagoon, where channels are deeper and currents stronger. Cows have been seen positioning themselves into ebbing tides, swimming just enough to match the speed of the water, their calves swimming continually in these situations as if on a treadmill, and likely gaining swimming endurance from these situations. As calves reach 1 to 2 months old they go into second-stage development where they interact with other young whales in social groups of twenty or more pairs. They interact physically, rolling and playing, and it is believed this serves as a socializing mechanism. The protective attitude of females to young changes after 2 to 3 months, when calves become more inquisitive and curious, approaching and playing with everything from kelp to boats. The third stage of calf development occurs just prior to departure from lagoons, with dramatically increased traveling activity, clearly in preparation for the serious business of migration.

The survival of newborns is hardly assured, as the discovery of dozens of dead calves along the shores of the lagoons is not uncommon. Causes of death include calves being struck by adult whales in mating groups; separation from mothers by males, strong currents, or vessels; and injuries from boats or fishing gear. About 5 per cent of gray whale calves of the year die near or in the lagoons, and another 30 per cent die in the earliest leg of the northern migration. Clearly the lagoon habitat is a safer place to be for the newborn.

Whales often approach quite close to boats.

Upwards of 20,000 gray whales migrate along the North American Pacific shoreline twice each year. They are northbound in the spring heading for summer feeding grounds and southbound in early winter heading for breeding lagoons. Much of the herd passes in a 6-week period, with hundreds of whales passing any one point during a day. It is one of the world's great wildlife spectacles.

The Longest Migrations

The shoreline migrations of gray whales up the entire coast of North America, into the Bering and Chukchi Seas, and even further into Arctic waters, is one of the predominant features of gray whale life. Twice annually passing population centers of California and the Pacific Northwest, where from coastal highways or residential areas anyone looking out to sea can see them, these are arguably the longest, strongest interfaces between wild whales and people. These journeys have often been described as the longest migration of any mammal. Some other whale species also make terrifically long migrations, but with a maximum 12,500 mile (20,000 km) round-trip, gray whales are certainly vying for the lead.

Sometimes, living on Vancouver Island and further north it is easy to forget there are two migrations — both northward and southward. There is the wonderfully close-to-shore, bright-weather, spring-time migration, which is near impossible not to see and is celebrated by many coastal communities with whale festivals and the like. Then there is the winter migration which mostly occurs in late November through December in the darkest, bleakest, stormiest months. In addition, it seems to occur slightly further offshore (still within sight of land), and the passage is of shorter duration, so it is not surprising that, other than in the southernmost legs of the trip, it passes with little human awareness.

As the summer feeding season begins to ebb, gray whales begin their southerly migration to Mexico. They start to leave the northern seas in late October and November, with a peak passage through Unimak Pass in the Aleutian Islands between mid November and mid December. Following the North American shoreline, most pass Vancouver Island in late December, Oregon a week or so later, with peak numbers passing California in the second week of January. The passage of the entire herd past one point takes about two months. An individual's journey may take about 6 to 8 weeks.

The migratory streams are segregated into age, sex and reproductive classes. Southbound it is led by late pregnant females, followed by non-pregnant females and adult males, and finally immature whales. Whale behavior during most of the southern migration has not been described due to the difficulty of observation in mid winter. Researchers conducting gray whale censuses in Unimak Pass in the Aleutians describe thousands of whales passing within a few miles of shore in November and December, then talk about the constant 40–70 knot winds, rain, snow and huge surf. During a study of migratory timing off Vancouver Island in the 1970s which asked lighthouse keepers to record sightings, one sighting form for December came back with the note, 'On about three days the visibility was clear enough to encourage us to glance out to sea and see the odd whale… at least that is how it would appear from our fog alarm report'. On those three days they saw 26 whales southbound. By the time the whales reach Oregon and California and better weather the early migrants are observed passing singly, then later pairs and groups of four more are common, the majority traveling within 3 miles (5 km) of shore. Descriptions of behavior within the southern migration are very scarce until the whales reach the southernmost leg and are nearing the breeding lagoons.

The return trip, the northward migration, begins in February with the first whales leaving the mating assemblies. In fact, the last of the southbound whales meet the first of the northbound whales of southern California. The northward passage then continues for months, with the last cows with calves traveling in May or early June. At peak times hundreds of whales pass any point through the day, with the majority of 20,000 whales passing in the peak 4 to 6 weeks. They migrate very close to shore, most within a few miles, some scraping along the shoreline rocks, or just outside kelp beds and breakers. With the long spring days it is spectacular, and no matter how much one reads about migrations, nothing comes close to seeing thousands of these animals in procession.

Gray whale mother and newborn calf migrating south; the calf has been born early.

The order of whales in the northward migration is newly pregnant females followed by non-breeding females, adult males, immature whales and finally in a separate late wave cows with young calves. The peak passage for the herd, minus cows with calves, is late February off California, mid March off Oregon, late March off Vancouver Island, and late April through Unimak Pass in the Aleutians. Following the main herd is a wave of cows with calves passing California through April and May, moving up migratory routes through May and June. The cows with newborn calves pass even closer to shore than the main herd, often within 650 ft (200 m).

The spring migration is anything but just a swim northward, certainly at least by the time it reaches Vancouver Island and the half-way point. Different whales, of different age, sex and reproductive classes, are all involved in different, perhaps critical, behavior patterns. There are whales on the outside of the migratory stream that are simply trucking, traveling steadily: three blows, a dive, then up a hundred or so yards further north, three more blows, dive and so on – making time.

On the opposite end of the scale are groups of up to five or six immature whales – mostly males, it seems – that are involved in social sex-play. These whales are found rolling over and alongside each other, penes extended, and at times wrapped around each other. Such groups meander northwards, at times covering no distance at all over a period of hours, and as little as a few miles a day. Other whales take breaks from the migration to feed on bottom sediments, in plankton swarms and on herring eggs. Herring spawn along the north-west coast coincides with gray whale migration. These feeding breaks may last from a couple of mouthfuls to a week or more. Other whales break from the migration to rub on sandbars, for unknown reasons, even if just for 20 minutes, then continue the trek. The late wave of cows with calves reach Vancouver Island in late May or early June, moving slowly along the shoreline, stopping to feed for a few days at a time, winding in and out of every little nook and cranny, seemingly in no rush whatsoever.

Gray whales swim at speeds from 2 to 6 knots depending on the activity and probably average about 4 knots during migrations. Due to the range of behavior patterns during migrations, including straight swimming, mating, play, resting and feeding bouts, migratory speeds are necessarily averages over time. It appears the whales speed up in the northern half of their migrations with estimates of northward whales covering about 40–43½ miles (65–70 km) a day off California and about 56 miles (90 km) a day further north. The whales apparently move faster when southbound, at an estimated 78 miles (125 km) per day. One whale radio-tagged in the breeding lagoons and tracked northwards up the coast by Dr Bruce Mate of Oregon State University provides wonderful specifics. It was tagged on 27 Feb 1979 in San Ignacio Lagoon, it passed La Jolla California 43 days later, was found off Oregon 61, 62 and 63 days after tagging and went through Unimak Pass, Aleutian Islands, 94 days after tagging. As it was still present in the lagoons on 14 March, the trip from Mexico to the Bering Sea took about two-and-a-half months. In traveling 4150 miles (6680 km) from the tagging site it averaged at least 20½ miles (33 km) per day from San Ignacio to San Diego, 50 miles (81 km) per day from San Diego to Oregon; 62 miles (100 km) per day for

Gray whales migrating north.

*Gray whale showing its flukes on a deep dive. During the migration north
some whales travel steadily towards their destination, others socialize and play making
very slow progress along the coast, and others take time out to feed along the way.*

A calf frolicking around its mother. Most cows and calves stay in the calving lagoons much longer than the single adults. They migrate in a separate wave a month or so behind the peak of the northern migration, and often travel very close to shore. Attacks from killer whales are a substantial threat.

two consecutive days along Oregon coast; then 79 miles (127 km) per day for the next 29 days to Unimak Pass.

Cows with calves, which have left the lagoons and are making their way up the coast, are perhaps most vulnerable to killer-whale attacks. This is not uncommon. In fact whalers felt, as related by R A Andrews in 1914: '…gray whales are the object of continuous persecution by killer whales…more so than any of the other large whales… if the grays are not paralyzed by fright they will head for shore and slide in as close as possible to the beach where sometimes killer whales will not follow… they will go into such shallow water as to roll in the wash and hide behind rocks…'

Calf – prey of killer whales.

Several researchers have felt that the reason cows with calves travel so close to shore and its kelp beds and surf zones is to mask their passage from killer whales. There have been several eye-witness reports of killer-whale attacks on gray cows with calves. In one classic case described by A Baldridge on 12 May 1967, the peak of the cow-calf migration off Carmel, California, a group of killer whales attacked a cow and calf. The attacks, centering on the calf first, took place outside of the kelp. The grays retreated into it for refuge. The killer whales took turns swimming over the calf as if to impede its progress. The calf was lost from sight for 15 minutes and when it was seen again it was dead. Killer whales fed on the carcass for at least three hours. When the 19½-ft- (6-m) long carcass was examined, virtually all the blubber from the ventral surface between the genital region and the throat had been removed, and the tongue had been eaten. The flukes and flippers had teeth marks, but were intact, suggesting the calf might have been held down and drowned.

Summer

During the summer months gray whales are found over an enormous range from northern California to the Arctic Ocean. Small populations spend the summer feeding along sections of coastline from California to south-east Alaska. The vast majority of the herd moves onto the shallow banks, and along the Siberian and Alaskan shorelines of the Bering and Chukchi Seas. The furthest rangers follow ice-free leads into the Arctic seas, seeping around as far as the Mackenzie Delta in the Beaufort Sea in northern Canada, and an equal distance over the top of Russia. In fact the gray whale feeding range extends over most of the distance of the migration.

Why some gray whales repeatedly move to feeding grounds just 620 miles (1000 km) from Mexican breeding areas, others to grounds 6200 miles (10,000 km) distant, is unknown. Most likely the density of food reflects the density of whales, and so most of the 20,000-plus herd occupy portions of northern seas where quality and predictability of food resources is greatest. Feeding can occur from March through December on the southern range and April through November in more northern sectors; a period of approximately ten months in the south and eight months in the north. Also, for females, the time spent feeding depends on their reproductive cycle. Newly pregnant females may be two to three months ahead of mothers with young calves in reaching feeding grounds in spring. Presumably females that are newly pregnant, and facing gestation, migration, birth and nursing require more food reserves than those that are near weaning their calf and feeding only themselves over the summer.

Gray whales are usually described as benthic or bottom feeders. They strain the sand or mud sea floor for several types of shrimp-like organisms, the most common being a particular type of amphipod. This activity is

Gray whale skim-feeding on plankton off Monterey, California.

dramatic. I've had the opportunity of watching gray whales feeding on bottom sediments from a few feet away underwater. After a few breaths they dip the head and on descent turn like a fighter plane, planting the side of the head with a slight forward thrust on the bottom and coming to a halt. Then with a powerful undulating motion, causing the expansion and constriction of the two or three grooves in the throat, they suction in a huge mouthful of sediment. Once full, and as the whale turns upright, a jet of sediment shoots out of the rear corners, sides and front of the mouth – presumably forced by the tongue. The food is sieved from the sediments by the baleen plates, which are almost like brushes hanging from the upper jaw. In the case I'm describing, it was a young whale feeding on small ghost shrimp living in mud bottoms. Whales will feed like this for hours a day for months. No other whale feeds on the bottom so often. In an area where grays have been feeding the bottom is pock-marked with around 3–6-ft- (1–2-m) long pits – whale bites.

On closer examination gray whale feeding gets even more interesting. Although bottom feeders at heart, gray whales feed on a remarkable diversity of prey types, and have an equal number of techniques to capture their food. They feed on the bottom, in the mid water column, and at the surface. They use suction, engulfing (taking huge mouthfuls), and passive filtering – simply swimming through the sea with their mouths open. They seem striking generalists in their diet, eating whatever is available. They remind me of coastal black bears on a foraging route. The bears may eat estuary grasses in spring or herring eggs on the beach; berries when available; crabs under boulders; salmon in the fall, or if a gray whale washes in dead, they will eat that. Over seventy different prey species have been recorded from the stomachs of gray whales. This is in contrast with other species of large whales like right whales and bowheads, which are relatively selective, and rely on just a few prey species. This propensity to eat almost anything may be one reason that gray

Gray whale skimming towards the camera, trapping plankton. Gray whales spend the summer on feeding grounds ranging from northern California, up the North American coast, and into the Bering, Chukchi and Beaufort Seas. If food is available many will start feeding on the northbound migration.

Gray whale passing through kelp. Although primarily bottom-feeders, gray whales prey on a large variety of planktonic as well as benthic organisms. They are often found in the midst of kelp beds feeding on huge swarms of a small 'shrimp-like' plankton known as mysids, which gather there.

whales, given any respite at all from hunting, have proven to be so resilient.

It may be that bottom feeding is the predominant activity in more northern seas, with plankton feeding more common in southern seas. Another view is that gray whales feed on a mixture of prey, moving from one prey type to another depending on abundance and quality in terms of caloric content – for example, choosing to feed on a species of plankton when it is carrying eggs. Vancouver Island grays may feed on herring eggs during the spawn period in early spring; then shift to a swimming amphipod that is swarming for a few weeks; then go to mysids that occur in huge blooms near kelp beds and surf zones for a month or two; then crab larvae that may occur in great densities through mid summer; then begin bottom feeding in the fall after the amphipods have had the summer to grow. It seems that it is an assemblage of species, all part of the coastal ecosystem that is important to gray whales, not just one main prey item. Grays leave an impression that they are tending a diversity of crops, harvesting the one that is ripe.

Summer feeding activity is broken only by bouts of traveling to another feeding area, resting, or a curious rubbing on sand bars and beaches. During summer, grays may range, or forage over hundreds of miles. At times they appear to check out three or four potential feeding locations over a few days, spending hours in each, then doubling back to return to the one that is best. The whales rest or sleep in several ways. Occasionally they lie motionless on the surface, waves breaking over them which, along with their color and no dorsal fin, make them look remarkably like rocks. Sometimes they lie in the midst of kelp beds just a few feet below the surface, rising to take a quiet breath every few minutes; at other times they slip into a resting swim pattern, slowly moving back and forth across a bay.

The function of rubbing behavior, beyond the well-known sensitivity of whale skin, and the likelihood that it just feels good, is not known. It may serve to dislodge parasites and barnacles, or dead skin. The whales have traditional rubbing places, there is one right in front of my house on the west side of Vancouver Island. It is a sand bar, 16–23 ft (5–7 m) deep, where whales rub regularly and, based on native knowledge, have been doing so for

Gray whales like to rub on the ocean floor.

thousands of years. The rubbing occurs both during migrations and in the summer. Whales will stop traveling or feeding and move purposefully to the sand bar and begin rubbing. They push themselves off the bottom, lying right side up or on their back, head rising above the surface, then 'falling' over to submerge for a few minutes before repeating it all. This can go on for minutes to hours, with one to five whales (including cows with calves) involved. This is just one of several such sites along the Vancouver Island shores, and one suspects there are many more throughout their range. It seems rubbing is as important to gray whales as it is to many other large mammals.

During the summer calves are weaned. Gray whale weaning occurs on the early side for whales, at seven months old or even earlier. Off Vancouver Island we find tiny whales, the year's young, alone by June and July. It appears from observations on the Siberian coast and Vancouver Island that once weaning occurs some degree of separation can exist between the young whales and the mature adults. Russian researchers report inshore areas, including bays and lagoons on the Siberian coast, that are almost entirely occupied by whales less than two years old, whereas adults are further offshore. On a much smaller scale, off Vancouver Island we find young whales in shallow mud or sand bays, or at times alone in kelp beds, with adults feeding in different habitats and locations. The small whale habitats provide greater protection than the open areas, and are rich in resources; huge swarms of mysid plankton in kelp beds, or dense aggregations of ghost shrimp in lagoon sediments, perhaps making them ideal nursery areas.

If one flew up the continental coastline and over the northern seas in summer, gray whales would be scattered over much of the route, over more than 6200 miles (10,000 km) of coastline. They would be in the midst of extensive kelp beds, around surf-swept rocks, in large sandy bays, mud-filled lagoons and on offshore banks. They'd be alone, or in groups of 20 to 30 on southern ranges, or in loose groups of many hundreds in the northern ranges. They might be trailing streams of mud where they've been sieving the bottom, or swimming, mouth open, on the surface through swarms of plankton, following tide-lines, or raising tail first in the midst of frothy, white water around rocks as they twist themselves into bizarre postures

Calf breaching on its birthing ground, soon to travel to feeding grounds thousands of miles away.

to push their mouths into crevices to suck in a mouthful of mysids. They are an integral part of our coastal ecosystem, both depending on and responsible for its richness and diversity.

Gray Whales and Humans

…friendly whales find you, you don't find them.
— S Swartz 1984

It is an understatement to say we seem pretty confused about our relationship with gray whales. At about the same time that hundreds were subject to Siberian 'aboriginal hunts' to be used as food for Soviet fox farms, three gray whales that were stuck in the Arctic ice were the subject of international rescue efforts; the scope, cooperation and cost of which was unprecedented. They were finally saved by the extraordinary work of a Russian ice-breaker. Further south, we love to watch gray whales and have developed a whale-watching industry that benignly pumps millions of dollars annually into local economies, yet we've decided to start killing them again. Meanwhile in Mexico, breeding whales are protected from tourist traffic, and San Ignacio Lagoon is declared a whale refuge and World Heritage Site; we are, however, entertaining proposals for massive salt mining operations that threaten this critical habitat.

This Jekyll and Hyde approach to the whales is actually progress. Our early relationship with gray whales was pretty straightforward. We killed them. Occasionally they killed us. Though events have been lost in time, this relationship was apparently fairly one-sided, resulting in, among other things, the loss of gray whales from the Atlantic. Early accounts of gray whaling leave the impression that it was pretty much war. C M Scammon noted in 1869: 'If the calf is wounded or killed, but not the cow she will in her frenzy chase the boats and overtaking them will overturn with her head and dash them to pieces with a stroke of her flukes…'; C H Townsend in 1886, '…if the calf was killed, the female, actuated apparently by motives of revenge, attacked boat after boat,

Three gray whales trapped in Artic ice spawned an international effort to save them.

63

demolishing it and scattering and drowning its occupants…'; or J D Caton in 1888, '…when it found itself pursued where escape was difficult, even before it was struck, it has been known to turn upon pursuers and dash a boat to fragments with a single blow of its powerful flukes, as so many a life has been lost'. These were the 'devil fish', the grizzly of whales. It is of course hard to know how much of this comes from our need to vilify them, considering the slaughter.

Curiously though, even in the midst of this onslaught, a clear fascination with the animals flows from anyone that spent time with them. A combination of awe and respect seeps out of the whaling accounts. These authors repeatedly refer to the cunning, courage, intelligence, trickiness, cleverness, affection for young, care for the injured and playfulness of the whales. It took near extinction, the subsequent disruption of the whaling industry, and a collective introduction to the living gray whales, for the other side of the human face, perhaps always present just below the surface, to emerge. The second phase of our recent relationship with grays followed.

The re-discovery by the public of gray whales passing San Diego in the late 1940s and 50s, and the familiarity with the living whales this brought, led to an unprecedented growth of our fascination and concern for these animals. By the 1960s this fascination had spawned a whale watching industry off California that showed the world that a benign, friendly relationship with animals could be, among other things, profitable. By the late 1960s they were advertising that nationally known marine biologists accompanied whale watching trips; and teaching modules based on grays were developed for San Diego schools. The acceptability of killing whales, for industry, research or aquarium entertainment quickly went right out of style. For the first time concerns were raised about the degradation of breeding lagoons and the need to protect their critical habitat. The aesthetic, educational and economic values of living rather than dead whales were recognized and acted on through laws and policy. The same inshore habits that spelled near disaster for grays from the whaling industry

The annual migrations of gray whales along the sea coast of North America are
hugely popular events. Whale watching from land and sea is a thriving activity, providing not only
enjoyment and educational opportunities, but an industry for many small coastal towns.

Since the mid 1970s a phenomenon known as 'friendly' behavior has
spread throughout the gray whale population. Gray whales of all ages approach boats
and carefully position themselves to be petted and rubbed – in some cases for hours
at a time. Here whale watchers and young whale meet in San Ignacio lagoon.

worked for them this time, and arguably began the phenomenal public connection to whales worldwide. A sea change had occurred.

As if to cap this new relationship, and at the far end of the spectrum of human relationships with whales, 'friendlies' appeared. In 1976 a gray whale in San Ignacio Lagoon deliberately approached whale-watching boats and allowed passengers to pet it. By 1977 this behavior was not uncommon, though restricted to a few whales in San Ignacio. I was there then, and was stunned to have a whale raising head first, 6 ft (1.8 m) above us, then gently leaning on our little rubber skiff, which was bumped and pushed about as the whale maneuvered so that we could pet and rub it. It was even more amazing to try to disengage and have the whale rush in front and stop the boat, intent on renewing the interaction. Initially most thought this was the exceptional behavior of a few young whales in the breeding grounds. But since, this friendly behavior has exploded through the San Ignacio population, then into other lagoons, then into the migrations and onto the feeding grounds. This has now become predominant behavior in the lagoons involving all sex-age classes and numbers: mothers with calves, males, females, groups of adults and immature whales, and single individuals. Some chronic friendlies spend all their time with boats and people rather than with other whales. They will follow boats for hours to resume friendly behavior at the first opportunity. This behavior is very exciting, and quite mystifying. By the 1980s virtually anyone in the lagoons could expect these encounters, and thousands upon thousands of people have now met gray whales on the closest of terms.

Our relationship with gray whales has changed in the last few decades, about as much as it could change. We have gone from killing them to kissing them. In stark contrast to our history with gray whales, we have come to see them as more than a carcass commodity. Beyond realizing a very profitable industry could be based on the living whales, we've perhaps begun to recognize their value to our world. We suspect they play key ecological roles in maintaining the diversity and health of our coastal ecosystems. We know they can teach us about the oceans. We may even make friends with them. Enormous strides have been made with the recovery of gray whales. The slogan 'Save the Whales' became symbolic of environmental awareness and the times.

However, times are changing. Gray whales continue to be hunted along the Siberian coast. The Makah natives of the Olympic Peninsula in Washington State, with the backing of the U.S. government and International Whaling Commission, have begun whaling again. Gray whales are now quarry on their feeding grounds and migratory route. And on the breeding grounds there is pressure to build a massive salt plant facility within San Ignacio Lagoon, the last semi-pristine gray whale birthing lagoon. All indications are this is just the beginning of new trials for the gray whale, as there are powerful pro-whaling forces at work worldwide. It seems we have a chronic split personality when it comes to whales. As we shift millenniums, human industry and politics are as much a threat to gray whales as ever they were, as these animals will face whaling, salt mining operations, oil and gas developments, fishing gear entanglements, and pollution. Ray Gilmore, longtime gray whale researcher and author, described grays in the 1960s as 'a relic species in a shrinking environment'. Perhaps, with all of our progress, this is still, inevitably, true.

It is this California population of gray whales that is often held up as the example of a conservation success story, of the ability of whales to recover from hunting. But with the perspective of the status of the other three populations it is a hollow declaration. It is perhaps a sign of our desperation to succeed in conservation issues, as we declared gray whales recovered and watched them taken off the endangered species list to be hunted again. We know the fragility of species. This is the last healthy population and we must look after it very, very carefully. Those of us living along the west coast pretty much take it for granted now, but indeed we are alone in the world with the option of having that fault.

*Makah natives of the Olympic Peninsula in Washington State
celebrating a kill. This was their first kill of a gray whale in 70 years and occurred
in May 1999. This continuing and highly controversial hunt has the support
of the U.S. government and the International Whaling Commission.*